The WEDDING DJ BIBLE

How to DJ the Wedding Like A Pro

From Preparation to Grand Exit !

by Neil Smith the Dandy DJ

Copyright © 2015 by Neil Smith Entertainment

Neil Smith Entertainment
2217 Sassafras Drive
Murfreesboro, Tennessee 37128
www.weddingdjbible.com
ISBN-13: 978-1519302335

Foreword -
You've Been Asked To DJ Their Wedding!
"Now What!?"

WHO THIS BOOK IS FOR -

Someone Who Has Been Asked By A Friend or Family Member To DJ Their Wedding - You may enjoy DJing as a hobby but maybe you have never done a wedding before and you really want to do your best! This book will guide you through everything you need to have, should be doing and exactly how to do it !

Brides and Grooms - who want to know what a wedding dj actually does besides just play music and what they should expect from a professional. They may also be considering asking a friend or family member to DJ their wedding and wish to give this guide to them as a gift to make sure they know everything they should be taking care of on the big day.

A New DJ - You're not quite sure what the ins-and-outs of a wedding are and would like to know where to focus and where to NOT focus your attention when trying to serve a wedding to the best of your abilities.

The Club DJ Who Has Been Asked To DJ A Wedding - There are very big differences between DJing clubs which generally focus on a very narrow demographic and DJ-ing a wedding which will typically have a very wide range of people from different ages and tastes in music. Also a wedding has a lot of different parts to the event which need special attention to be conducted in the correct way.

WHAT THIS BOOK IS AND IS NOT -

What This Book IS
This book is a step-by-step guide on everything a person needs to have, know and do in order to prepare and conduct the services of a professional-level wedding dj in a clean, confident manner.

What This Book Is NOT
This book is not an instructional on how to land clients.

Now get ready to read, learn, work hard and have fun

ABOUT THE AUTHOR

Neil Smith, the DANDY DJ is a full-time professional wedding DJ located in Murfreesboro, Tennessee serving the Nashville market and has also spent many years serving the Los Angeles, California market before relocating to Middle Tennessee.

Neil has spent many years fine-tuning his service to couples celebrating the most special day of their lives and loves to share what he has learned, mostly through trial and error (lots of error). Hopefully this book will serve to shorten your learning curve through the benefit of Neil the DANDY DJ's experience.

CONTENTS

Chapter 1: Equipment - 17 Things You Will Need

In this chapter, I will go over the minimum equipment you will need in order to provide proper service for a wedding.

1. Insurance

This is very important for a variety of reasons. There are some venues who will not even allow you on their property unless you have insurance. Also, because you are moving somewhat heavy equipment in and out of a place where there is likely to be frail elderly people, small children and alcohol combined with dancing, the potential for an accident is great enough that you really should be carrying insurance. My personal insurer is R.V. Nuccio which runs about (at the time of writing this) around $280 per year for $2m general liability. If you are a member of a professional organization such as the American Disc Jockey Association, it drops to less than $200 per year.

2. Music Library

To operate legally, your music must be licensed for public performance. There are many resources to obtain music inexpensively which will allow the legal replay such as Promo Only, Content Unlimited and cheapest of all would be a record pool. You can learn all about these various methods by joining some DJ groups on FaceBook. There are advantages and disadvantages to most every resource, so you'll want to choose accordingly depending on your own budget and needs.

3. Music Player and Backup Music Player

You need to have a device to actually play the music from. My best suggestion would be a laptop. Actually the best suggestion would be two identical laptops which are exact clones of each other in case one has problems, you just switch to the other. If you are operating on a super tight budget, then I suggest one laptop and at the very least, carry a backup copy of your entire music library on an iPod which you can plug in and at least continue playing music should your laptop fail. You should be using some proper DJ software. Some cheap and free but stable ones are Virtual DJ, **DJay**, **Serato**, Mixxx and even iTunes can be used effectively if configured the right way.

4. Mixer

This can be as elaborate as a multi-deck controller to work your DJ software program with or as simple as a small 4-channel mixer which you can find for around $65 at a music store. The main thing is, you want the ability to plug your music player into it (preferably 2 music players) along with at least one microphone. I personally use the Behringer Xenyx 1002B Mixer because in addition to having multiple channels to work with, it can also run off 9v batteries which makes it very useful for ceremonies in an open field or on a beach where electricity is not available.

5. Speakers

Your speakers should at the very least be 12" speakers, preferably 15" and should have a horn. I also suggest you purchase powered speakers which carry their own amplification. These are much more versatile and can be used without needing to be plugged into the rest of your system and are not much more expensive, especially when you consider you will be saving money over needing to purchase a power amplifier if you should instead purchase non-powered speakers (passive speakers). The speaker I personally use for receptions is the JBL Eon G2 and the speaker I use for ceremonies is the Samson Expedition XP40i Rechargeable Battery Powered PA.

If you aren't familiar with the terminology I am using here, you should visit a music store and simply look around and let the salesperson know what you are looking to do and your budget range but don't purchase right away. You are just there gathering ideas. Once you identify some speakers you like, in your budget range, you will want to go do some research before buying. Look the speakers up online and read consumer reviews from a variety of sources. Once you have found a pair you like in your budget range, you can either order online, or if you really felt comfortable with the personal relationship you built at the store, purchase at the store.

6. Speaker Stands

You will need to also buy a pair of tripod speaker stands capable of easily holding the weight of the speakers (about $80 a pair for the cheaper ones). My experience with the cheaper speaker stands is that the clamping knobs (a long screw bolt with a turning knob on one end which tightens the stand) and the nuts they screw into tend to wear out within a couple of months. I have had great luck finding replacement clamping knobs and nuts of much better quality at Tractor Supply and hardware as well as other hardware stores. Once retrofitted with the replacement parts, I have NEVER worn one out since. You can retrofit a stand for about $5. PS - The replacement nuts are usually slightly larger than the hole in the stand they are meant to fit into. Some gentle persuasion with a hammer will fit them right in. The speaker stands I personally use are OnStage Speaker Stands.

7. Speaker Cables

Of course you also need to buy cables to connect the speakers. There is no need to buy complete top of the line cables as you won't be worried about the utmost fidelity in a setting such as a wedding (there will be a lot of ambient noise from conversations, laughter, etc.) but you should buy cables that will have some durability which you can also easily unscrew the ends from for when you will inevitably need to repair the connections at the end at some point due to natural wear. In music stores, I have personally had better luck with the quality of cables from Sam Ash Music Store rather than Guitar Center. Many people however swear by ordering cables online from MonoPrice.com for the best quality at a low price. Be sure to get extra cables as well in case one goes bad at the event. Be sure to have a couple that are 50ft in length and a few that are around 20ft in length. The three main types of cables for speakers are xlr, 1/4" and speakon. You'll need to determine the type that is used for your speakers.

8. Hand Cart

You need something heavy duty to haul your equipment safely into and out of the venue. The Cadillac of carts at the time of my writing this is the Rock N' Roller Hand Cart which can be a stand up hand cart or a flat rolling cart. This is one area you don't want to skimp on quality. Get something durable that can fold down small and carry a lot. You'll be glad you did! I personally use the Rock N' Roller R8 cart, but you should research and find the one that best suits your needs.

9.   Microphone   and Backup Microphone

At a wedding, there will be some announcements you will be expected to make such as calling guests to be seated, the grand entrances, introducing the special dances, introducing speeches, cake-cutting, bouquet, garter, last dance and grand exit. You will need a microphone, preferably wireless. If you're trying to save money, I have personally had great luck with VocoPro microphones, particularly the VocoPro UHF 3205 2 microphone package. They are rugged quality, rechargeable and sound good while resisting feedback (squeal when someone holds the mic too close to a speaker). You want to have an extra microphone on a different frequency ready to go in case the other gets interference (it happens! I once was using a wireless microphone for somebody's speech and suddenly Yellow Submarine from the Beatles started coming through my system because a band down the hall was using the same frequency). I have since switched to a wireless microphone system that is a bit more expensive that has the capability of scanning multiple frequencies to choose the strongest signal with no interference. These days I use the Audio Technica System 10.

10. Table

A table is a standard piece of equipment that every DJ should carry. True, many venues will provide a table for the dj, but you never know what they are going to have or if they will have anything at all for you. For about $45, you can pick up a 2' x 4' table that has extendable legs to make it cocktail height, perfect for standing and working, at Costco or Sam's Club or just order one online from Amazon or eBay. Ideally, you want exactly the amount of space you need to work with and absolutely no more as you don't want guests to be encouraged to set their drinks on your table, **which brings us to the facade**.

11. Facade

A facade is basically a decorative wall which can either be a tabletop facade (which sits atop the table and provides a protective and aesthetic wall between the guests and your equipment) or a full facade which is much larger and hides your entire table (much more expensive and cumbersome). This will help prevent people from knocking into your equipment on the table and especially will help keep them from holding their drinks over your laptop and mixer while they requests songs (but don't be surprised when they still come right over the top of the facade with their drinks. It's just one of those things you must constantly look out for and deal with as a DJ). I made my tabletop facade from screen window frames painted black with white spandex rolled in place of where the screen material would go. This allows me to place lights behind it and really make it look amazing! A great pre-manufactured tabletop facade would be the Grundorf Tabletop Facade.

12. Tablecloth

It is important to always look your best. Your table should always be draped with a proper tablecloth and it should extend all the way to the floor to hide your wires and connections. Large black tablecloths run about $10 each at WalMart.

13. Formal Wear

Yes, your clothing is a part of your equipment! If you are a male, it is customary to wear a black suit, white shirt, black tie - preferably a bow tie. For a female, formal wear that's not overly-flashy but comfortable to work in. I'm a guy, so I will leave that one there. I would not suggest loading in and setting up in your formal wear but instead carrying that in a garment bag and changing in the restroom once finished setting up. **My key tip on clothing** - I wear black Dickies **work pants** instead of dress slacks. People cannot tell the difference and because I am climbing to put speakers on stands and also on my hands and knees to route cables, I need pants that are tough enough to take a beating while still looking good. Early in my career, I had a continual problem with ripping the crotch in my dress pants during setup. Since switching to wearing Dickies, I have not had a problem in several years.

14. Dance Lights

It is usually expected that a DJ will provide some sort of lights which will add color and movement to a dance floor. I strongly suggest using led lights which put off very little heat. It will make your life much easier. On the low end, you can find a set of 4 lights which will be sound activated and provide your color and movement, for around $200 (I got mine from Eliminator Lighting). The stand for a small set of lights will run you around $80. Start small and work your way up. I personally use the Eliminator Electro 4 Pack with an inexpensive 9 ft. tall t-bar stand that I personally retrofitted with pin inserts for extra safety and stability. Unless you are handy with retrofitting metal equipment stands, I suggest that you spend just a little bit more and get something along the lines of the Odyssey Tripod Stand w/ T-Bar.

15. Gaffers Tape

It is important if your cables will need to go across any doorways or walkways that they be taped down for safety purposes. Gaffers tape is a special kind of tape which holds securely but comes up cleanly, therefore not ruining the floor which could get you in a lot of trouble and cost your client their security deposit, which will in turn get you in a lot of trouble! Gaffers tape is about $20 per roll, but used conservatively should last quite a while.

16. Extension Cords and power strips

You won't always have the luxury of having all of your powered equipment conveniently placed right next to electrical outlets, so you'll need to be prepared. Carry some heavy duty extension cords of at least 14 guage, preferably 12 guage (the smaller the number, the beefier and better at delivering power they are) and make sure to have at least 100 ft. You'd be surprised at just how short a 50 foot extension cord actually is once you are trying to reach power from across a ballroom or lawn without routing it directly across the dance floor.Black is the best color as it will blend in more settings. You'll also need some professional-grade power strips with surge protection. You'll generally want to have twice as many outlets as you think you'll actually need at your disposal. You'll quickly be surprised at how quickly they fill up, especially if you are plugging in any of those bulky wall-worts that can cover more than one outlet. It's good to use power strips that space the outlets apart to account for this and also that have the outlets positioned perpendicular (sideways) to the strip.

 **17. Two Pens and a Notepad**
Over the course of the event, people will come up to you with announcements you will need to make and it will be important to take notes. Be sure to carry a couple of pens with you in case one runs out of ink.

If you haven't caught the overriding theme of this chapter yet, it's to **have backup for EVERYTHING** *because when something goes wrong or a piece of equipment fails (and believe me, when it happens, it will happen at the worst possible time), it is absolutely crucial that you be ready with a backup you can pull out at a moment's notice to get through the event with.*

Chapter 2: Preparing The Music

This chapter assumes you already have legally obtained the music you need and have it fully downloaded to your system.

Be Legal But Avoid Copy Protection

First off, while I want you to be legal, I also want you to avoid music files that are copy protected because this can make it difficult to create multiple backup safety copies which you really need to have just in case.

iTunes For Organizing

I find the best system for organizing music, while I'm not exactly an Apple fan, is iTunes (the program, not the store). In fact, you could actually DJ an entire wedding with this program because it allows you to cue up your next songs to play and will even fade them over for you. If you are starting on a very small budget, I wouldn't personally think twice about simply dj-ing right from iTunes, but this chapter is not about performing, it's about preparing, so I digress.

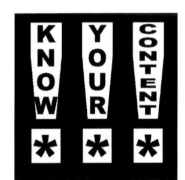 ## What's In Your Music?

Before adding music to your library, it is important to know what's in the music, meaning language and content. You want to obtain clean versions of songs or "radio edits" but even then, if they are singing about smoking pot or having freaky sex, it's probably not the best thing to play at a wedding where you will have children and grandmothers in attendance. Be sure to look up the lyrics on the internet before adding to the wedding's playlist. This takes time but it's what you get paid to do. You are ultimately responsible for the content that comes out of your speakers.

If a song contains explicit language, I would rename it to read "*Song title (explicit)*."

If it doesn't contain explicit language but does contain content which may be inappropriate for some audiences, I will rename it "song title (mature)." I personally take the extra step for popular songs with explicit language and questionable content of pulling them into an editing software program and editing out the bad words and content if feasible.

If a song is so raunchy that it simply cannot be edited clean at all, I do not add those into my library period and have wording in my contract that states I will not play music containing explicit language or extremely raunchy content. For the small minority of people I will please by playing raunchy music versus the other hundred or so I stand to offend, it's simply not worth it to ruin my reputation as a provider people can feel safe trusting their families with. Use your own best judgment and proceed with caution.

Making It Foolproof - How To Label Your Playlists

When I'm doing a wedding, I like to minimize my chances of making mistakes in every way possible. With the music, I do this by creating a special iTunes playlist for each and every portion of the event and putting those playlists in order.

iTunes automatically puts playlists in alphabetical order which unfortunately doesn't really help in this case, so what I do is every playlist will start with the date of the event followed by a letter repeated 3 times (because triplicated letters do not appear anywhere in the English language) followed by the name of that segment of the event.

Below is an example of how I name my iTunes playlists to keep them in perfect order:

081515 aaa CER Prelude
081515 bbb CER Bridesmaids Aisle
081515 ccc CER Bride Aisle
081515 ddd CER Candle Lighting

081515 eee CER Recessional
081515 fff Cocktail Hour
081515 ggg Grand Entrance
081515 hhh BG First Dance
081515 iii Dinner Music
081515 jjj Father Daughter Dance
081515 kkk Mother Son Dance
081515 lll First Song Open Dance
081515 mmm Open Dancing
081515 nnn Cake
081515 ooo Bouquet
081515 ppp Garter
081515 qqq Last Dance
081515 rrr Grand Exit

As you can see, I have the entire wedding mapped out and in order and doing it this way will keep these playlists at the top of your iTunes in perfect order. Obviously, some playlists will only contain a single song such as the Bride's aisle walk. This is ok. The point is to have an easy to follow guide and to make it almost impossible to make a mistake.

You're trying to get all your thinking done ahead of time and make everything almost automatic on the big day so you come off as flawless!

Chapter 3: Setting Up

Arrival Time

If only doing the reception, I normally arrive about two hours prior to my starting time to allow time to load in, setup, make everything look sharp, route cables as inconspicuously as possible, drape my speaker and light stands to hide the cabling going to them, tape down any cables crossing walkways, put away all equipment cases, fully test the equipment and get the sound right, change into formal wear and give a final review of the timeline before service begins. Also keep in mind that you will likely have people from the bridal party, venue, coordinator, etc wishing to go over last minute details with you during this time and it will eat into the time you have to get everything dialed in. You must be prepared to give these people your time and attention when needed and this is a big reason why arriving two hours prior is so important. If I am also servicing the ceremony, I will add an extra hour onto my overall setup time and arrive 3 hours prior. Remember, Anyone can show up one hour prior, slap it together and be functional but look like a slob. The goal here is to make you stand out from the crowd. You want to make magic and wow the people you are there to serve. This requires extra time and attention to detail that the other DJs don't care enough to give.

Staying Safe

Accidents happen usually when you are trying to do too much too fast and get reckless. Mama was right - lift with your knees, not with your back! Don't pile too much equipment on your hand cart. Make multiple trips. Be extra careful when and if standing on a step ladder. Also don't forget to tape down any cables that must cross walkways with gaff tape to hold securely and come up clean at the end of the event.

Stashing Cases

After you've unpacked everything you need, try to consolidate your cases and bags down to the smallest footprint possible. Fit as much inconspicuously under your table as you can. If there is a place to stash your cases out of sight inside the venue, as long as you can't be locked away from them, take advantage of it.

Second choice would be if it's convenient, take your cases out to your vehicle.

Third choice would be if you have room, neatly stack your cases behind your area if room allows but cover them with a black tablecloth to make them inconspicuous and blending in and finally, if you are parked somewhere inconvenient but there is simply no other choice, sometimes you do need to grunt it out and just haul your cases back to your vehicle and that's just the way it goes. Just part of the job.

Testing Everything

Once you have everything set up and BEFORE you drape your light and speaker stands or tape cables down, be sure to test everything such as your main and backup music players and microphones to make sure everything is functioning properly and sounding good. Make any needed final adjustments at this time.

Making it Pretty

Remember, PEOPLE HEAR WHAT THEY SEE !

This means that you can make the sound more amazing than anything anybody has ever heard, but if they walk in and see a sloppy mess, none of that will matter because all they will perceive is how unprofessional and disheveled your presentation is.

Hide your cabling. Drape your stands to hide the wires, make sure your tablecloth extends all the way to the floor to hide what's underneath and any equipment casing, cart, stepladder, etc that can't be stashed inconspicuously beneath or behind something, be sure to cover with a black tablecloth to make it look neat and hidden.

*** PRESENTATION IS EVERYTHING! ***

Chapter 4: Ceremony

Yes, believe it or not - at many weddings, the DJ serves the ceremony as well as the reception, usually with a separate smaller-scale setup if in a separate location from the reception.

Since the ceremony is a very quiet setting, the slightest thing wrong will stick out like a sore thumb unfortunately, so this is one area of the occasion where the pressure is really on! The slightest microphone crackle or not having the microphone on when the officiant begins to speak, the slightest missed cue with the music, since it is a very quiet and focused time for all attending - every imperfection is instantly magnified !

Meet with the Officiant Prior to the Ceremony

This is important because you want to know where they will want to stand (sometimes it seems obvious and then the officiant will just walk up and change everything, so don't skip this step). You will want to test the microphone from the position from which the officiant will stand. whether it be a microphone on a stand or a wireless lapel microphone. If it is a microphone on a stand, after testing you will want to mute this microphone from your control area so it doesn't pick up extra noises such as wind if you are outside or footsteps from the wedding party walking down the aisle if inside (hardwood floors will reverberate right through the mic stand and come through very loudly in the sound system, so keep microphones muted until the moment they are needed!). Also be sure to ask the officiant to be careful not to hit the microphone stand with their book (or electronic tablet) as this makes a horrible and loud clunking noise.

If the officiant will be using a wireless lapel microphone, be sure to place the transmitter on the side of their body nearest to the wireless receiver and also instruct them to not have their cell phone on the same side of their body as the transmitter or allow the wire from the lapel mic to come anywhere near their phone. This can cause interference and you will hear a sort of morse code electronic sound come through when this happens. It does not sound good. Also be sure to inconspicuously hide the receiver for the wireless unit as close to the officiant as you possibly can for the best signal and then simply run a signal cable from that over to your control area. I normally tape the receiver to the top of a microphone stand and find a good place to hide it. Also be sure to instruct the officiant not to make any big arm movements as this will cause their clothing to rub against the microphone which sounds exactly like white noise interference and your client will believe your equipment is at fault.

One final point to go over with the officiant is to identify the very last thing they will do before you are to begin the recessional music. This is usually where they turn the bride and groom to face the seated guests and announce the newlywed Mr. and Mrs. _____. But be sure to touch on this as they may have something different worked out and you don't want to start the music at the wrong time. You can't undo it once it's done.

Pre-Ceremony Announcements

Call to seating / Silence Devices - Once you have called guests to come be seated in the ceremony area (if that duty falls to you) be sure to make a few trips about five or ten minutes apart from each other in front of the altar to thank the guests for coming and also to ask them to please place any electronic devices on silent at this time. Since people will be continually arriving and being seated, you'll want to repeat this a few times during the prelude (the portion before the start of the ceremony). This is also a great method of testing the microphone and making needed adjustments to the tone and volume when people are present.

Coordinating the Aisle Walks

If there will be a coordinator keeping things on track, you will want to make a plan with them to receive cues on when to change music for the different aisle walks. Normally the coordinator will stand near the area where the bridal party will be walking from and you'll be able to set up some hand signals for when to start the aisle walks and when to change the aisle walk music from the wedding party over to the bride's aisle walk. Be sure to do your due diligence beforehand and know the exact person in the bridal party who will be the very last person to walk down the aisle before the bride. Often when the coordinator or even the bride will tell you who this person is, quite often they will forget about the flower girl and ring bearer, so make sure once again ask after they tell you "Ok, this is the VERY LAST PERSON that will come down the aisle before the bride? No flower girl? No ring bearer?" You would be shocked at how many times after I repeat the question in this manner I have seen a light bulb go off over the bride, groom or coordinator's head and they'll say "Oh yes!" And then correctly tell me who the last people will be. You don't want to play the bride's music for the wrong people! That's a huge mistake you cannot undo! If there is no coordinator, then you just look for the last person you have already identified as being the final person before the bride in order to know when to change the music over to the bride's aisle walk. Be sure to fade out the music, give a few seconds of silence (not too much) and then quietly bring in the bride's aisle walk, gently increasing volume from that point if needed. It's better to start too soft than too loud. When the bride reaches the top of the aisle, if all the guests are still seated and the officiant fails to ask guests to rise (it happens), politely call out "All Rise" just one time. When the bride nears the altar, gently fade the music out. DO NOT - I repeat DO NOT make her stand there waiting for the entire song to complete. That is very awkward and obnoxious and I have heard many tales of DJs doing just that.

Tweaking the Sound

During the ceremony, you may notice that people will move closer or farther away from the microphone than you had envisioned or that one person may be a very low-talker while another will have a very loud and booming voice. You will need to stay focused and ready to make gentle adjustments throughout the ceremony in regards to volume and tone.

Staying Alert

Keep your wits about you, especially if there are any special portions within the ceremony that will require special music such as a sand ceremony, unity cross, candle lighting (I have even done weddings with celtic hand-fasting and even the bride and groom washing each other's feet while I was asked to read scripture). Also while there are ceremonies that last a long time, there are others that are over and done in five minutes and you really don't want to miss starting the recessional (music that is played as the bride and groom walk away down the aisle together) upon their announcement! Stay focused and DON'T MISS YOUR CUES!

Post Ceremony Instructions

Once the Bride and Groom, the wedding party, parents and grandparents have made their aisle walk exits, at this time you will usually need to lower the music so that the officiant can instruct guests on where to proceed next. If the officiant does not make this announcement, this duty will assuredly become yours!

Transitioning from Ceremony to Reception

The very next thing you want to do is retrieve your lapel microphone from the officiant if you used one, then get music started in the reception area (start the dinner music playlist and let it run on it's own) then get back to the ceremony area and pack up and put away your equipment from that area as quickly as you possibly can. The bride, groom and wedding party are normally out taking pictures at this time so you will usually have about 30 minutes to get this done. Sometimes more, sometimes less, but be sure to poke back into the reception area regularly to adjust sound and make sure everything is going fine. If my vehicle is nearby, I usually just place all the ceremony equipment right into my car. If not, then I bring it to the reception area and consolidate it and hide it away wherever I can with the focus being on making everything neat, presentable and inconspicuous!

Chapter 5: Grand Entrances!
The Big Ta-Da!

The Grand Entrance is where the Bride and Groom as well as their entire wedding party (usually) make their "Grand Entrance" into the reception. It is the DJ's / Master of Ceremony's job to announce each individual entrance as well as to play the appropriate music.

The List of Names

Quite often, the client will provide the list of names to announce. This is a nice reference but **DO NOT - I repeat... DO NOT trust this list under ANY CIRCUMSTANCE** as it will almost always certainly change. People don't show up, can't be found, decide they don't want to be part of the entrance, other people will be added last second, the flower girl and ring bearer will suddenly be napping on mom and dad's shoulders, etc, etc.

Instead, when the wedding party arrives, put the cocktail / dinner music on autopilot and walk out to greet them. at this time, you will line them up in the order they are to be introduced.

This order is usually as follows:

* Bridesmaids and Groomsmen
* Flower Girl and Ring Bearer
* Maid of Honor and Best Man
* Bride and Groom

Notice how the hierarchy builds up until you arrive at the most honored.

You want to go down the line and ask them each to say their names while you write them out phonetically for yourself (how the names sound as opposed to how they are spelled). This will help you avoid mistakes. Also be sure to write in big, bold letters as the area you will be announcing from may be a bit dark and if it is not, somebody may last second get the brilliant idea to darken it for effect!

When you finally arrive at the Bride and Groom, ask them (even if they have already submitted it to you) how they would like to be announced. When they tell you, write it down and show it to them and ask if you have it correct.

Once approved by the Bride and Groom you next ask a couple of key questions if you haven't already been issued this information (but it is still good to re-verify things because assuredly it has been a hectic and event-filled day for all involved, things could have changed and nobody thought to inform you).

First Dance Right Away or Later?

Verify if the bride and groom will immediately go into their first dance or if they will simply enter, wave and then go straight into the meal (the latter is tending to be more common these days).

Blessing The Meal - Yes or No?

Ask at this time if there will be anyone saying a blessing over the meal and if so, who will you be inviting up to give the blessing. If they will be going straight into their first dance, also ask if they will be doing the parent dances immediately afterwards as well. Once these events begin, you will not have another opportunity to find out until it's too late, you're on and suddenly you have no idea what you should be announcing. You don't want to be a deer in the headlights. Once again, all of this may have been sent to you beforehand, but on the big day things will tend to change last minute and everyone will have been told except for you. Be thorough (but be extremely polite during this).

Final Instructions

Once you have these key questions answered, it is time to give the wedding party their final instructions before entering. The most important instruction is to make sure they understand **not to enter until they hear their names called,** otherwise they walk in, you say their names and the people behind them come in the door and it appears as if you are announcing the wrong people (I actually tell the wedding party the reasoning and I get much better cooperation when they understand why). Then I ask them to give me a minute to get things cued up and ready for them.

Are The Caterers Ready?

If the meal will begin immediately after the grand entrance, I personally make sure the caterers are ready. This is important as I have been told by coordinators more than once to announce the meal and the food wasn't ready. The result is that I appeared as if I didn't know what I was doing and those were very embarrassing moments. It actually happened to me twice - two weddings in a row (and I have not let that happen to me again since!)

Once the meal is verified as being ready, you want to get the grand entrance music cued up, ask all guests to find their tables and then begin the grand entrances!

Do it with energy and have fun, and if you have followed everything up to this point, it should go smoothly and you should look like the awesome pro you already know you are!

Chapter 6: Dinner Hour, Speeches and Toasts!

Most DJ's (and clients) think the dinner hour is the portion where the DJ is the least needed and is normally regarded as the DJ's break time. This couldn't be further from the truth!

The Dinner Hour

This is the portion guests have been waiting for hours to arrive at! They have been traveling, dressed up, escorted, directed, sat through a ceremony, moved again, directed some more, have been having conversations left and right and honestly, they are ready to sit and have a bite to eat.

All this is true BUT they still have a long time to go at this occasion, wish to have their energy kept up, they wish to stay entertained AND THEY ARE A COMPLETELY CAPTIVE AUDIENCE! This is a portion of the celebration where the professional level DJ gets the opportunity to rise above and truly shine!

If the family is religious, the meal will normally begin with a blessing done by a family member, good friend, sometimes the minister (if the ceremony was performed by a minister) and I have even had couples ask me to bless the meal on occasion. If this is something you aren't comfortable with, you'll want to have a courteous response of something like - "This is such a special moment, I really wouldn't feel right. Could we ask for a family member or someone very close to you?"

If saying the blessing is something you are comfortable with, be prepared but be mindful of others in attendance that may not share the same faith as the bride and groom, keep it short and respectful. Use your best judgment.

Buffet or Table Service?

If the meal will be table service, be sure to let the guests know that their meals will be out shortly and to please enjoy each other's company.

If the meal will be self-serve buffet style, **ALWAYS** invite the head table (the wedding party) first, led by the bride and groom unless the bride and groom are being served (this should be determined beforehand of course), then announce to the rest of the guests that you will be coming around and inviting their tables to the dinner line and to please stay at their tables and enjoy each other's company until you come by (and if tables of guests completely ignore you and get in line anyway, be sure to keep a smile on your face and continue releasing tables in an appropriate manner. There is nothing you can do about rude guests, but you can occasionally repeat your polite announcement that you will come to the tables and invite them and to please remain seated until you come around). If you know where the closest family are seated, make a point of starting there with the dismissal of tables and be sure to do it in person at the table and **NOT OVER THE MICROPHONE.** Calling tables over the microphone cheapens the experience and makes the guests feel as if they are at a fast food restaurant, not the most special gathering of a family's life! **NEVER FORGET** that this family has usually spent thousands of dollars to celebrate in style and have trusted you to **KEEP THINGS CLASSY!**

Normally the closest family will be seated nearest the head table. Always try to dismiss the tables with the parents and grandparents first and work your way out from there, keeping an eye on the food line and dismissing tables one or two at a time. Be sure to know if the plates will be at the food line or if the guests need to bring their own plates from their table's place setting.

Be sure to keep music playing during this entire time on automatic play on a dinner music playlist you have prepared in advance. It is important to keep the music upbeat and familiar so the guests aren't nodding off in their plates. It should be loud enough to hear, but quiet enough to easily allow conversation.

Once all the guests have received their meals, this is usually a good opportunity to make your own way through the food line. Be sure to keep your plate behind your setup and out of view. Remember, you are always to keep things classy, right and tight!

SPEECHES AND TOASTS

After about ten minutes or so of the guests enjoying their meals, it is time to connect with the coordinator, or if there is no coordinator, the bride and groom about the speeches and toasts which are normally given during the dinner hour because it is the only time for the rest of the gathering you will have everyone captive in their seats and somewhat quiet and at their best behavior (not completely drunk yet). You'll need to determine the names of the people speaking and their relationship (i.e. Father of the Bride, Maid of Honor, Best Man, etc.) and the order they will speak so you may introduce them properly. Many couples will give you this list in advance, but in my experience this will often change as a best friend may ask to speak, or a grandparent or someone else near and dear to the couple that they hadn't planned on. Also some who were supposed to speak will sometimes get cold feet and decide they really don't wish to. This is why you always want to determine the speakers at this time of the event.

One last thing about speeches and toasts - Always wait a moment after the glass has been raised before announcing the next speaker as they will usually take a few seconds afterwards to hug the couple, shake hands and pose for a quick picture. Your job is to keep things moving elegantly, but don't rush   it.

Chapter 7: First Dance, Parent Dances, Special Dances

The reason I put this chapter here after the dinner, speeches and toasts portion is because I'm finding more and more, the special dances are happening after rather than before, usually from a desire to allow the guests to get their meals without any further waiting. I'm finding this to even be the case more often than not when the first dance and parent dances were actually scheduled to happen immediately upon the grand entrance. They realize the guests are getting hungry and do a last minute change to get them fed. It may just be a regional thing here in the Southern United States but since that's what I have to go from, there you go.

Before The Special Dances

Before you get into the special dances, make absolutely sure everybody who will be participating in these are present and accounted for (Bride, Groom, Parents) and are ready to get into this portion. You do not want to make the mistake of announcing someone who is not even in the room! I've made this mistake before and it made me look awkward like I didn't know what I was doing and even worse, it made things a little embarrassing for the people being announced as it made them feel as if they were holding things up by not being present when they were being announced over the microphone. Also, make absolutely sure you have all the special dance songs cued up and ready to go. You don't want to be fishing for them after the announcement or have your focus anywhere else once these dances begin in case you get a signal from the floor to cut the song short (happens all the time).

BRIDE AND GROOM'S FIRST DANCE

When you have made absolutely sure that everybody is ready, you may announce the Bride and Groom's First Dance. You'll want to say something along the lines of "Everybody, let's please bring our attention to the dance floor and give a warm welcome as it is time for the Bride and Groom's First Dance!" My best advice on this is to start the volume low and gently fade it up to an appropriate level. You want to be careful not to start the song too loud as it can be shocking to the couple as well as the guests since the sound is beginning immediately following a period of silence in the room (yes, I've made this mistake before as well and practically blasted the bride and groom right off the floor with the first few notes of the song! It was very embarrassing and needless to say, I never made that mistake again!).

Never EVER speak over the microphone during the special dances, just don't.

Also be sure to keep your beverage and food out of sight as the photographers will be taking a lot of pictures during this time. You may very well end up in some of these pictures and you want to be sure to appear engaged and alert in them when your clients (and potential future clients) view them later!

Dance Light Timing

I will normally wait until the chorus of the Bride and Groom's First Dance before I kick on the dance lights. I have found that this adds a really nice impact as the energy of the song reaches it's first key part. Also, you want the photographers to be able to get a good amount of pictures without the dance lights so they can more easily create some of their own effects in their editing process without having to edit around various multi-colored lights. Remember, you are not the only provider your client has spent good money on. Be sure to do everything you can to help them get the best value from everyone they have hired. The better their overall experience, the more favorably they (and their guests / potential future clients) will be remembering you!

Ending The First Dance

Stay alert and keep your eyes on the dancing couple as in my experience, after a couple of minutes, especially if it's a long song, they will sometimes discreetly motion to go ahead and wrap up the song. When and if this happens, simply lower the volume of the song and invite guests to give them a big hand and keep the song playing softly while you announce the next dance. If the couple dance the entire song to it's conclusion, invite everyone to give them a nice round of applause as the song ends and ask the bride to remain on the dance floor as you invite her next dance partner to the floor for the...

PARENT DANCES

Father / Daughter Dance

Since the focus of the event is normally on the bride more than anyone else, the next special dance is usually the Father / Daughter Dance.

When it comes to the parent dances, you want to be careful with the announcements as the person coming to dance may possibly be a step parent (and the biological parent could possibly be in the room!). If you know for certain that the person joining the bride for the Father / Daughter Dance is indeed considered to be the father, a great way to invite him to the dance floor would be something along the lines of "Dad, please come to the dance floor, it is time to dance with your daughter on her wedding day! This is the Father / Daughter Dance!" Be sure to wait until Dad is in place and ready before starting the song.

IF THE FATHER FIGURE IS A STEP-PARENT OR OTHER RELATION - DO NOT USE ANY REFERENCES TO THE RELATIONSHIP! Instead, you'll want to invite them to the floor in a manner such as "I'd now like to invite Mr. Johnston to the floor to share this special dance with our lovely bride!" Apply this same method of announcing for the Mother / Son Dance if the Mother figure is a step-parent or other relation. This is one portion of the event where emotions and sensibilities can run high if the family is extended, especially if tension exists. You want to be very careful to tread lightly, speak in generalities and be sensitive.

Mother / Son Dance

Once the Father / Daughter Dance has concluded, be sure to invite everyone to the give them a round of applause and invite the groom to escort his Mother, or if not the Mother, his "very special dance partner" to the floor and observe all the same protocols as you did for the Father / Daughter Dance.

OTHER SPECIAL DANCES

First off, make sure the Bride and Groom have indicated they actually **WANT** to have these special dances before just doing them. Some couples love these, others don't care for them and would prefer to simply go straight into the open dancing once the parent dances have concluded.

Money Dance

The Money Dance is a lot of fun and very entertaining for everyone if done the right way. AND if done the right way, does not come off as trying to extract money from the guests at all, instead it becomes like a game.

You invite the Bride and Groom stand at opposite ends of the dance floor and then invite the male guests to line up for the Bride and the female guests to line up for the groom and have at least a dollar (no coins) ready. If the Bride and Groom do not have satchels to receive the money in, ask the Maid of Honor and Best Man to receive the money as people approach the Bride and Groom for the dance. Let the guests know to not wait for the entire song and to instead just walk up and tap the shoulder of the person dancing in front of them after a few seconds and politely cut in. Since you've already had the slow, sensitive moments with the First Dance and Parent Dances, you'll likely want to have this music upbeat and fun. You'll start noticing ladies lining up to dance with the Bride and the Groom's male friends lining up to dance with him as a joke and this is where the real fun begins. The Money Dance, in my experience usually lasts about 3 songs before it has run it's course.

Couples Dance

This is my personal favorite! Announce that the Bride and Groom have requested that before the open dancing begins, they would like **ALL COUPLES** to come to the floor for a special dance. Then wait a moment and ask if you have them all (you really want to be sure to have the oldest married couples for this one). Make sure you have a popular romantic song ready to go that's at least 3 minutes long. You then announce "Ladies and Gentlemen, this is something we like to call THE COUPLES DANCE and it goes a little something like this..." (begin the music).

"If you are a couple on the dance floor and not even dating, please leave the dance floor at this time!"

"If you are a couple on the dance floor and you are ONLY dating, please leave the dance floor at this time"

If have been married less than 4 hours, please leave the dance floor at this time!" (obviously the Bride and Groom now must leave the dance floor)

"If you have been married less than 6 months, please leave the dance floor."

Keep proceeding with one year, two years, five, ten, fifteen (increments of five from this point forward) giving a good ten seconds between announcements to allow people to enjoy their dancing a bit and be sure to invite applause for the couples remaining who have made key milestones such as the five, ten, twenty and twenty five year marks and keep going until only two couples remain, then use your best judgment to go by single or multiple year benchmarks until you have only the longest-married couple remaining, then lower the music, bring them the microphone and ask them to give the newlyweds a piece of advice for a long and happy marriage (or at least a long one). Have everyone give them a round of applause and then announce that the **DANCE FLOOR IS OPEN!** (and then kick up a song that is a sure-fire dance floor filler - quickly! Usually a participation dance like the Cha Cha Slide or the Cupid Shuffle will be something that's a can't-miss!)

Chapter 8: Open Dancing

Kick Starting the Dance Floor!

Normally the best way to get a dance floor going is if you have the Bride and Groom come out to the floor along with the wedding party to help get things started. You'll want to announce to have everyone join the bride and groom on the dance floor because the dance floor is open! Then start with something that's sure fire, upbeat and has universal appeal to get everyone up and having a great time!

*(**PLEASE NOTE:** The following musical guideline is simply what has proven to work well for me in most of my wedding situations for the demographics I typically serve. These may or may not be a good fit for the type of demographics you are serving. Once you have enough experience, you will usually be able to read the crowd and adjust accordingly. Until you have that experience, getting a list of requests from the Bride and Groom in advance is the best place to start and also be sure to announce to the guests to feel free to make requests and that you will be "happy to play them if you are able." This wording does give you an out in case you are asked for a song you simply don't have or if you are asked for something inappropriate.)*

I will usually start with a participation dance (unless I have been specifically asked NOT to) such as the Cha Cha Slide or the Cupid Shuffle and will also get out on the floor myself to lead the dances and get things going. This "almost" always works very well (there are no certainties and sometimes you need to adjust quickly and adapt if you see something is not working as you thought it would).

After a couple of participation dances, people will usually have had their fill of them for the time being and you'll want to start shifting the energy. This is usually a great time to transition into a good danceable universally-appealing mid-tempo classic (Brown Eyed Girl or similar), after which you can announce a couple's dance where you can play a couple of slow dance numbers. Classics almost always work best as they will draw the most people, young and old to the floor. Great choices I have found to work well for me are "Let's Stay Together" by Al Green, "Unchained Melody" by the Righteous Brothers and also "My Girl" by the Temptations. Once again, adjust for your crowd as needed.

Also remember that the people you see currently on the dance floor are not necessarily the only people in the room

wanting to dance (a good number of folks may simply be on the sidelines waiting for a song that fits their style) and you'll want to be mindful to play some music that those not currently on the dance floor will enjoy (and possibly make their way to the dance floor once they hear it). Don't be afraid to change things up a bit with different styles and if you see people really enjoying something in particular, add more of that, but be careful not to beat it to death.

Tempo Flow

You want to keep things upbeat and energetic, but you don't want to wear out your crowd. They need breathers every so often. I will usually flow the music with about three upbeat songs, one mid-tempo, one or two ballads (depending on the response), one mid-tempo and back to the upbeat songs. I use the mid-tempo numbers to act as buffers between the fast and slow songs so the shifts aren't so abrupt. I find it normally creates the best flow. Be sure that the mid-tempo songs are very popular and very danceable, but that should be true of all the songs you choose. Remember, you are not there to play YOUR favorite songs. You are there to serve your clients and their guests and to help them have the best time possible.

Taking Requests

Absolutely take requests unless specifically instructed not to, but if someone requests a song that you know will completely ruin the dance floor, use your judgment and wait for a good moment when dancing isn't the main focus or when there is a noticeable lull to throw it in. If the person requesting is the bride, groom, immediate family or a member of the wedding party however, make that request a priority and get it on as quickly as possible unless the request is simply inappropriate (i.e. foul language, raunchy content), then simply state that you don't have it.

Keeping Things Appropriate

Remember that a wedding is a family event. You will have grandmothers, children and people of many types in attendance. Therefore it is very important to keep things appropriate in regards to the language and content of the music you are providing. I personally state upfront in all my marketing and also in my contract that I will not under any circumstance play music with explicit language or raunchy content. This ensures that I only end up serving clients that wish to keep things clean. You'll need to check your own moral compass as to how far you are willing to bend on this one.

What To Do If You Receive An Inappropriate Song Request - Simply state you don't have that song.

If A Guest Hands You Their Own Music Player!

If a guest tries to hand you a phone or other device (hard drive, etc) to play songs from, simply state you don't have the ability to play anything from an outside device. Playing songs from a guest's device is very dangerous because you have no idea what could come out of it through your speakers, much less if it is even a reliable playback device (a disc could be scratched, skipping or unreadable, their phone may have a bad output jack, a hard drive could contain a virus or incompatible formats and probably a hundred other pitfalls I'm not even thinking of right now!). You are ultimately responsible for the content and quality of what comes through your system and should absolutely know exactly what you are playing and the reliability of the playback devices you are utilizing at all times. Playing anything from a guest's device is not something I would personally do under any circumstance ever.

The "Do Not Play" List

Sometimes a bride and groom will include in their list of requested songs a DO NOT PLAY list. This is common and should always be respected and adhered to without exception.

If The Bride and Groom's Requests Aren't Danceable

This happens sometimes and you simply work their must-play songs in wherever you can while also doing everything you can to please the guests. You will usually want to wait until you've had people dancing for at least a few songs and have shown your success at getting people onto the floor and also make sure the bride and groom are in the room and hopefully close to the dance floor when you play them. Any non-danceable songs they have requested that will work for the dinner hour, be sure to play them during that time and for the rest, just slip them in whenever you see a good opportunity and cross them off your list as you go.

If You Receive A Super Loooong Playlist! or... What To Do If The Bride's Submitted Playlist Is Longer Than You Could Ever Possibly Play In The Course Of The Event!

This happens all the time. I will receive a list of 100+ songs a week before the wedding (the timeframe that I ask them to have their list of special songs submitted to me by) which is far more than could ever possibly be played in the course of several weddings. This is usually the result of the bride and groom sitting around having fun and planning their special night and just making a list of all their favorites and simply not realizing that it would be completely impossible to play everything from a list this extremely large (if you played music nonstop, the average number of songs in an hour would be around

18). You simply make sure you have all of their songs prepared, play as many of the non-danceable ones during the cocktail and dinner hours as possible and for the open dancing portion, give priority to the most popular and danceable selections first. Play the others when you can or as requested.

Chapter 9: Cake, Bouquet and Garter

Cake Bouquet and Garter are typically done together after about the first half hour of open dancing although sometimes the bride and groom will choose to cut the cake much earlier in the night directly after dinner so their guests may immediately enjoy their dessert. Sometimes this decision can be made very last minute, so stay alert and be flexible. Sometimes the bride and groom will choose to do the cake, bouquet and garter very early in the event so they may dismiss the photographers and videographers early in order to save money.

If you get about a half hour into the open dancing portion and nobody has given you any indication (planner, family member, wedding party member, bride or groom) that they are ready to cut the cake and do bouquet and garter, be sure to seek out the bride and groom and politely check with them to find out when they would like to get into this part of the event. They may actually be waiting for you to initiate this, so staying in communication (without being overbearing) is key.

CAKE CUTTING

When you get the thumbs up to transition into the cake-cutting, first make absolutely sure the bride and groom are in the room (yes, sometimes a planner or wedding party member can tell you they are ready to do the cake and not realize the bride and groom have stepped out for a breath of air for a few minutes! How embarrassing would it be to announce the cake cutting and the guests of honor aren't even in the room!? How unprofessional would you appear?). Once you have determined the bride and groom are in the room, lower the music and announce to everyone that it is TIME TO CUT THE CAKE and to please feel free to gather around and take pictures but to please not get in the way of the professional photographers.

If the bride and groom have chosen a special song for the cake cutting, obviously play it at this time. Otherwise, songs about sugar and sweetness work best. Some great choices can be "How Sweet It Is To Be Loved By You" (either the James Taylor or Marvin Gaye versions), "Sugar, Sugar" by the Archies, "Sweet Thing" by Keith Urban, "Sweetest Thing" by U2 and "Sweet Thing" by Van Morrison. These are the ones I have had requested most often. You might want to avoid the song "Cut The Cake" as I have not had a good response to this the couple of times I have tried it. If the bride and groom end up smashing the cake into each other's faces and making a mess, be prepared to stretch things for a few extra minutes afterwards to allow them time to clean themselves up and also so the bride may find her bouquet for the upcoming toss.

BOUQUET TOSS

First make sure that the throwing bouquet has been located! You wouldn't believe how often a coordinator or a bridesmaid will ask me to move into the bouquet toss and then suddenly I see an entire wedding party running around in a panic trying to find the missing bouquet. Be sure to ask if the bouquet has been located before moving into the toss.

When you get the thumbs up to get the bouquet toss underway and all systems are GO, invite all the "UN-MARRIED LADIES" to the dance floor because it is time for the BOUQUET TOSS! This wording is important because if you ask for the "single ladies", some with boyfriends may not think you are calling for them. It is important to be literal. Have fun with this but don't draw focus away from the bride. This is her big moment. If she has chosen a special song, play it at this time, if not - three songs that have worked well for me have been "Single Ladies Put A Ring On It" by Beyonce, "Man! I Feel Like A Woman" by Shania Twain and "It's Raining

Men" by the Weathergirls. Once the bouquet has been caught, ask the lady who ended up with it to join the bride for a picture with the photographer and to stay around until after the next portion.

GARTER

Depending on the sensibilities of the bride and groom, they may or may not wish to do a garter toss. Make absolutely sure in advance that they indeed wish to do one before announcing it. Once you have determined they do wish to do the garter, you'll want to have two songs prepared - one for the removal and one for the toss.

Garter Removal - Bring a chair out to the middle of the dance floor and invite the bride to have a seat. No need to announce the garter, everyone will automatically know what it is for. It is important that you let the bride and groom's interaction lead this portion and be very careful to not say anything which may come off as inappropriate. Songs that have worked very well for me during the garter removal have been "Bad To The Bone" by George Thorogood, "Highway to the Dangerzone" by Kenny Loggins and "Let's Get It On" by Marvin Gaye.

Garter Toss - Once the garter has been removed, it's good to announce "Let's give our lovely bride a kiss as she makes her way off the dance floor and let's also please clear the chair away while we call all the unmarried guys to join us out in the center!" The guys will usually take a bit longer to come to the floor than the ladies in my experience so feel free to encourage the crowd that if they know an unmarried guy who is present and not coming to the floor to bring them out. Once you have all the guys on the floor, you'll want to change over to the garter toss song. My go-to for the toss is usually "Eye of the Tiger" by Survivor but as with most of my song suggestions, you'll want to use your own judgment about what will work best with your style and the tastes of your clients and do what works best for you. After the garter has been caught, ask the guy who caught it to join the bride and groom along with the lady who received the bouquet for a special picture with the photographer and let everyone else know that the dance floor is once again open!

Chapter 10: Last Dance and Grand Exit

Last Dance

The Last Dance may be written in the timeline (usually for about five minutes before your scheduled ending time) but while you are in the final dance set of the event, be sure to have the last dance song ready to go at a moment's notice. Quite often the bride and groom will have had a very long day by that point and it is not uncommon at all for one of them or one of their parents or a maid of honor or best man to walk up and give you the word that they are ready for the last dance a half hour or sometimes even an hour before your scheduled ending time. You don't want to keep them waiting in this case. You want their final impression of you and your services to be that you were on the ball every step of the way.

If it gets to be about fifteen minutes until your scheduled ending time, be sure to connect with the bride and groom as they will have been having fun this whole time and may have lost track of the time. You don't want the ending of the night to blindside them and you certainly want them to be in the room and ready to dance when you announce the last dance. If you are fortunate, they may decide they may not be ready to end the party and want to retain you for extra time.

When the time comes for the last dance, be sure to announce that it is indeed the last dance and invite everyone to the floor to send our newlyweds off in style. If you have been given a certain song to play for the last dance, of course play it, but if not, my opinion is that when left to your own devices, play a romantic ballad for the last dance for two reasons: 1. To make it really special for the bride and groom and 2. To help bring the energy of the room down to minimize hyped up people from screaming for you to keep playing music once the last dance has finished. The bride and groom have indicated this is when they want you to be finished by, you have a long teardown, pack up and load out and the venue wants you off the property in a timely fashion (and believe me, you are more than a little likely to be the last one to leave).

Grand Exit

Once the last dance has concluded, ask everyone to give the newlyweds a nice round of applause, and if a grand exit has been coordinated, go ahead and invite everyone to the designated area to give a fond farewell to the bride and groom. Sometimes the grand exit will include bubbles or sparklers. If so, be sure to let everyone know to grab those on their way out to the sendoff area and then play whatever song has been requested for the grand exit, or if left to your own devices, be sure to play something with a theme of going away, but somewhat upbeat. (perhaps something along the lines of "I've Had The Time of My Life" or similar).

And while people are exiting the room and you have the music playing, start breaking down anything you are able to immediately. It's also during this time, that I will usually take my timeline that I have worked from and write a nice thank you note to the bride and groom on it and place it with their cards so that later as they read through them, they will come across the nice sentiment I wrote them and remember me fondly.

Chapter 11: After The Wedding – Teardown, Pack Up, Load Out, Follow Up

Teardown

Be sure to teardown things in an orderly manner and keep your things out of walkways or off of things that are being packed up by other people as best you can and be very careful to do it SAFELY. By this time you have had a long day and if you have served your client well, you should be tired. You want to take extra caution when removing your speakers from the stands and handling other heavy objects as people are likely to be scurrying around trying to get their own items packed up and some of them could also very well be intoxicated. You want to be extra careful to keep your most sensitive and expensive equipment (such as your laptop computers) very securely away from any place someone might step on them, spill a drink on them or otherwise stumble into them and be sure to get those in their proper cases ASAP. You want to be working as quickly as you possibly can during this time as you will likely be the last vendor to leave the venue and you don't want the party responsible for locking up to be waiting for you any longer than they have to.

Pack Up

I usually designate a certain area for everything that has been completely packed up and this usually helps keep things in good order and helps me to minimize fumbling around. You want to pack things away neatly and not just throw things in bags and cases to sort out later, that way you are ready to go for your next event. The pack up is the portion of the event where it can be very easy in your fatigued state to damage a piece of equipment in your rush to go. Damage the wrong piece of equipment and sorry to say, but you just lost every dollar you made. You do want to work fast, but methodically and carefully. Never haphazardly.

Load Out

Once your equipment has been properly packed in it's cases, If it's safe (as in weather, area where you won't be robbed, etc.) go ahead and just get all your equipment out the door, hopefully to an area you can pull your vehicle up to. This way, the people in charge of shutting down the venue can go ahead and get the doors shut and locked behind you. On your last trip out the door, be sure to take and extra good look around to make absolutely sure you haven't left anything and also be sure to pick up not only all of your garbage (tape, cup, note paper, etc.) but also any garbage that anyone else may have left in your area to make sure that you do not leave an impression that you have left a mess for others. Whether it was your mess or not is besides the point because the venue is likely to believe you made the mess. You want to be in good graces with the venue, not only because it's the right thing to do, but because they could also be a great source for future business. Then get your vehicle, pack it as quickly and safely as possible and exit the property immediately but driving cautiously. Remember, absolutely everything you do from the moment you arrive to the second you are gone is leaving an impression on people who may be able to help your future business in some way. Don't ever lose sight of this. It is so easy to lose business you simply don't know you have lost.

Follow Up - Thanking Your Client and Requesting A Review

The following day, be sure to send a nice email to your client thanking them for allowing you to be a part of their special gathering. If the bride and groom had come up to you at the end of the event giving you hugs and handshakes and obviously completely thrilled with your service, then also ask your client for a review in this email letting them know that it helps others to have confidence when considering using you. Be sure to have some place they can leave reviews, preferably a third party website that you cannot control the content of. This gives proof to your future prospective clients that your reviews are real. You can set up a page on Google for people to leave reviews, also Wedding Wire. If your client isn't particularly internet savvy, they may just email their review to you and then you would just publish it on your own website.

By this same token, if the client did not give **ANY INDICATION** as to how pleased they were at the conclusion of the event, **DO NOT** I repeat **DO NOT ASK THEM FOR A REVIEW!** You never know what could be in another person's mind or what sort of experiences they may have had at the event that you may not have had anything to do with, but still may somehow get attributed to you. Things like this are simply beyond your control sometimes. One bad review carries the weight of a hundred good reviews and you want to avoid negative feedback on the internet in every way you possibly can.

So once again, **ONLY ASK FOR A REVIEW IF THE CLIENT IS GOING ABSOLUTELY HOG WILD OVER YOU AT THE CONCLUSION OF THE EVENT! NO EXCEPTIONS!** Otherwise, simply thank them for using you and let them know that if they ever need anything else, to please not hesitate to contact you again. If after that, they reply on their own cognizance letting you know how awesome you were, at that time you may ask them to post a review about your services online.

This concludes our book! Happy DJ-ing !

Thank you for reading, now get out there and serve like the pro you are!

Neil Smith, the DANDY DJ
www.dandydj.com

THE END

51643284R00060

Made in the USA
Lexington, KY
05 May 2016